Chanukah & Purim

An Exposition of Jewish Law and Thought

Rabbi Yair Hoffman

Chanukah & Purim

Dedication in Memory of
The author's parents
Dr. Nathan & Sara Hoffman ob"m

Table of Contents

Chapter One - Chanukah

1. Chanukah occurred during the time of the Second Beis HaMikdash in 3621 or 140 BCE. The Seleucid Greeks (or Syrian Greeks) ruled and enacted decrees against Klal Yisroel – outlawing their religion. They forbade Torah study and the observance of Mitzvos. Ironically, these Greeks knew what many Jews do not know – that what makes Klal Yisroel unique is Torah and Mitzvos. Without these, our spiritual existence would gradually disappear and we would no longer be the Am Hashem.

2. The Greeks took our money and violated our Bnos Yisroel. They entered the Mikdash and desecrated it. They polluted that which was pure and caused Klal Yisroel much distress. The Greeks placed such stress on Klal Yisroel that Hashem finally had compassion upon us and rescued us. The Chashmonayim, the Kohanim HaGedolim, were victorious in battle against the Greeks and saved Klal Yisroel from their hands.

3. The Chashmonayim installed a king from the Kohanim – restoring the monarchy back to Klal Yisroel for more than 200 years - until the destruction of the Second Beis HaMikdash (3829 or 70 CE).

4. The date that Klal Yisroel was victorious over the Greeks and destroyed them was the 25th of Kislev. That day they entered into the Heichal and did not find any pure oil in the Beis HaMikdash with the seal of the Kohain Gadol – all except for one flask of oil. That flask contained enough oil to last only one day. They used it to light the lamps of the Menorah and it lasted for eight days. It lasted long enough for them to crush olives and extract pure oil.

5. Because of this Nais (miracle), the next year, the Chachomim of that generation decreed that these eight days, beginning with the 25th of Kislev, should be days of Simcha and Hallel.

6. On these days, during the evening, we light Chanukah menorahs at the entranceway of our doors to show and publicize the miracle. We do so for all eight nights.

7. Nowadays, most people light by the window because there is more Pirsumei Nissah, publicizing the Mitzvah, if it is in the window rather than at the

doorway. All this points to the idea that a small measure of light can push away much darkness.

8. These days are called Chanukah because "Chanu" – they rested from their enemies– on "Kah"- the 25th. Kah in Gematriah is 25.

9. The Nais that we celebrate is about the oil and not about the military victories. The reason for this is that the Chachomim of the time were concerned that people would think the victory was because of the military tactics of the Chashmonayim and not because of Hashem's Divine intervention. The Chashmonayim did end up relegating to much power to themselves as well. Because of this error, some of their descendents did not follow the ways of Torah, and the country was divided in civil war. This is another reason why it is the oil that is commemorated.

10. Also, the miracle of the flask of oil hints to the continued existence of the Jewish people throughout the darkness of the Golus – which is a miracle in and of itself. No other nation in the world ever existed in exile for so long and eventually came back to their land. This miracle is attested to in the first Rashi of Sefer Bereishis – Hashem started the Torah with Bereishis Barah so that in the future when the gentiles accuse us of stealing their land – we can say that Hashem

created the world and gave the land to us. This Rashi was written over 900 years ago. The continued existence of Klal Yisroel, particularly in the land of Eretz Yisroel where the gentiles are now accusing us of stealing their land is truly remarkable. This Rashi is an inspiring Nais.

11. The Beis Yoseph, Rabbi Yoseph Karo, asks a famous question about Chanukah: Why do we celebrate Chanukah for eight days instead of seven? The miraculous extra burning was only for seven days! This question is known throughout the Torah world as "The Beis Yoseph's Question." There is a book that has over 500 answers to this question!

12. One answer is that even though technically the miracle of the oil lasted for only seven days, since there was enough oil to last one day - we still celebrate Chanukah for eight days because the victory itself is deserving of its own special day – just like Purim has a day. It was also the day that they found the oil – so Chazal decreed that the Menorah be lit on that first day too.

13. Another interesting question that is often asked about Chanukah is: Why did the Chashmonayim wait until they got pure oil? There is a halachic concept called "Tumah Hutrah BeTzibbur" – if needed for the

Tzibbur - impure oil may also be used! They could have used the impure oil as well. Why didn't they?

14. One answer that is often given is that the Chashmonayim were setting things up for the first time after a long period of disuse. In such circumstances everyone is looking and observing. The Chashmonayim taught us not to settle for things that are impure – but to do it in the best possible manner. This is a lesson in Chinuch too, to teach that one should always strive for the highest level.

15. It is also quite curious why there is no mention of the obligation to light the Chanukah Menorah anywhere in the Mishna. Indeed, the only mention of Chanukah in Chazal is in Megilas Taanis which pre-dates the Mishna and in the Gemorah in Shabbos 21a. The Chsam Sofer explains that since Rebbe Yehudah HaNassi, the compiler of the Mishna (about 1800 years ago), was a descendent of Dovid HaMelech – he left out the miracle involving the Chashmonayim – since they should not have taken the Malchus for themselves but should have left it for the descendents of Dovid HaMelech. Indeed, the Ramban writes that Hashem punished the Chashmonayim for this act. We had a civil war amongst ourselves and eventually the Bais HaMikdash was destroyed.

TIME OF HAPPINESS

16. There is a very ancient book in Torah sh'beAl Peh that was written even before the Mishnayos were written down. It is called "Megilas Taanis" and was written when the Beis HaMikdash was still in existence. This book listed many lesser holidays - joyous days and sad days that we Jews celebrated. After the second Beis HaMikdash was destroyed we stopped observing all of these other days, because Chazal tell us "there was no more joy." The Talmud Yerushalmi (2:12) tells us: All of the special holidays were set aside except two holidays - Chanukah and Purim.

17. On these days we may not give a Hesped – a eulogy at a funeral. Eulogies make people sadder and we may not do that on Chanukah. There is an exception for a Talmid Chachom – if the aron of the deceased is present at the funeral.

18. We are also not permitted to fast on these days. Fasting makes one sadder too, and this is not permitted on Chanukah. We cannot fast – even if it is for the Yartzeit of a parent. However, we are permitted to work and perform Melacha.

19. Women have the special custom not to do work while the Menorah is still lit. The reason why women

have this custom is because a woman - Yehudis, the daughter of Yochanan the Kohain Gadol, brought about a miracle. She was very attractive and told the persecuting king that she would be intimate with him. She fed him dairy products so that he would be thirsty. He drank wine and got sleepy. She was able to kill him and cut off his head which caused the general of the army and his soldiers to all run away.

20. Since this miracle occurred through dairy foods – we have the minhag to eat dairy foods on Chanukah. We should have in mind when eating dairy of the miracles that Hashem did for us.

21. There is a Minhag to eat Latkes on Chanukah. This is because they are fried in oil in order and commemorate the miracle that happened with oil. This Minhag is mentioned by the Rambam's father. In Eretz Yisroel, donuts are also eaten for the same reason.

22. There is also a Minhag to play with a dreidel on Chanukah. This commemorates the Mesiras Nefesh of the children for Torah study. The Greeks forbade the study of Torah. When the Greeks checked on the young students who studied Torah anyway, they pretended they were playing games. The dreidel also signifies that the instigation of help during the time of

Chanukah started from Hashem Above – not from us, the spinner is on top. On Purim, the move toward Teshuvah came from us down below – which is why we use the grogger.

23. There is also a Minhag to distribute Chanukah gelt to family members and children at this time. This is to create the joy that will enhance the appreciation of the Nissim Hashem did for us.

24. Many Poskim (including the Vilna Gaon) are of the opinion that there is a slight Mitzvah to increase feasting on Chanukah – because on these days the work for the Mishkan in the Midbar was also completed then. If we add zmiros to these meals they would be considered a Seudas Mitzvah. If there are no zmiros they are not considered a Seudas Mitzvah.

25. The Ramban in BaMidbar (8:2) quotes a Midrash on the Posuk "When you kindle the lamps" – the Torah here is hinting to the events of Chanukah.. When the Leviim saw that the Nesiim of each tribe were bringing dedication offerings and the shaivet of Levi did not [and were sad], Hashem said.."There will be another Chanukah [dedication] where there will be a lighting of lamps when I will perform miracles.. for Israel.. The sacrifices are brought only as long as the

Bais HaMikdash will exist..but the lamps [Chanukah] give light forever.."

26.Chanukah is a time in which we give greater Tzedakah (Mogain Avrohom) because it is a time of Geulah – redemption.

GENERAL ASPECTS OF LIGHTING

27.One must be very careful in regard to lighting the Chanukah menorah. If one is careful, the reward is children who are Talmidei Chachomim. According to the Shulchan Aruch, even a poor person supported through charity should collect money or even sell his clothing in order to light. This is the only Rabbinic Mitzvah that has such a requirement. Indeed, even many Torah Mitzvos do not have such a requirement!

28.Why is this so necessary? Because the Chanukah Menorah does two things:

a. It publicizes the great miracle that occurred.

b. It also serves to increase praise and gratitude to Hashem for the miracles He has done for us.

29.With the lighting of the Menorah we reinforce the concept that all of Creation, and the life force of every living thing is because of Hashem's Will. We state that Hashem will, at times, intervene with His laws of nature when He so wills it. We acknowledge that Hashem is the true source of salvation and we express our sincere gratitude for the miracles He performed on our behalf in the time of the Chashmonayim.

30. Since the Chanukah Menorah acts in such a capacity, it is important to focus on increasing our praise and gratitude toward Hashem. The gratitude extends to our own lives as well – not just during the time of the Chashmonayim.

31. One can fulfill a Torah obligation when lighting the Chanukah Menorah. The Torah Mitzvah one fulfills is "VeNishmartem meod lenafshosaichem" (Dvarim 4:15) – that one must take safety precautions and protect oneself and others. Fire is extremely dangerous and many people have been injured or killed r"l when proper safety measures were not taken regarding Chanukah candles. Otherwise the Mitzvos of Chanukah are Derabanan.

32. The obligation to light is called "Chovas Ha-Bayis" – it is upon the house – not the individual. Homeless people not staying in a house are technically exempt. Even though the obligation to light is on the house, the main obligation falls upon the Baal Ha-Bayis.

33. A person should attempt to be home during the time of the lighting and to light the candles himself. This is because of the concept of Mitzvah Bo Yoser mibeshlucho – it is better to perform a Mitzvah oneself then through a messenger.

34. If the wife knows that the husband will be coming home – she should not light for him until midnight – because he is the main householder and the Mitzvah is greater for him than for her. Once midnight has arrived, however, she should light the candles. It is also appropriate to gather the entire family around to light the Menorah – even if there will be somewhat of a delay in lighting. If most of the family members are home then one or two children who arrive later should light on their own and not delay the rest of the family.

PROHIBITION OF DERIVING BENEFIT

35. It is forbidden to derive any benefit (Hanaah) from the Chanukah lamps or candles. One cannot read next to them or use the light for any other purpose. There are two reasons for this prohibition of Hanaah.

a. Rashi explains that everyone must see that these lights are only for one purpose – to publicize the Miracle.

b. The Ran explains that since these lights comme-morate the Menorah that was in the Bais HaMikdash – the same halachos of the items of the Bais HaMikdash still apply – no benefit may be derived from these items.

36.It is for this reason that we make sure to also light a Shamash in addition to the candles. If one did use light, halachically, we assume that the light one inadvertently uses came from the Shamash. The Sha-mash should be placed in a different area than the regular Chanukah lights so that it not be confused with the Chanukah lights themselves.

37.The candles or the oil placed in the lamps must be enough to last ½ hour. If someone lit a Menorah that did not have enough oil in it, he or she should relight the Menorah, but without a new blessing. There is no extra hiddur – beautification of the Mitz-vah in putting a lot of oil in the lamp.

38.There is a debate in the Gemorah as to whether the placing of the Menorah does the Mitzvah (Hanacha oseh Mitzvah) or the lighting does the Mitzvah (Had-lakah oseh Mitzvah). We rule that Hadlakah does the Mitzvah. Therefore if one lit the Menorah in a place that one would not have fulfilled the Mitzvah (such as above twenty Ammos) and then moved the Menorah later – the Mitzvah has not been fulfilled and he must relight.

THE PROCEDURE OF LIGHTING

39.The basic obligation of Chanukah is just to light one lamp for the entire household each night of Chanukah. The Mehadrin – those that go above the basic obligation, have everyone in the household light one lamp each night of Chanukah. The Mehadrin Min HaMehadrin – those that go above and beyond have everyone in the household light two lamps on the second night, three on the third night and four on the fourth etc. The custom all over is to light like the Mehadrin Min HaMehadrin.

40.How do we actually light? The Chanukah Menorah is set up in the place that provides maximum Pirsumei Nissah, publicizing the miracle, but is still safe. The entire family is gathers around for the lighting so that there is more Pirsumei Nissah. The candles or lamps are arranged from right to left on each night, but they are lit from left to right.

41.There is a debate between Bais Shammai and Bais Hillel as to how we light. According to Bais Hillel we light one candle on the first night, two candles on the second night, three on the third etc. According to Bais Shammai we light eight candles on the first night, seven on the second night, six on the third night etc. Even though we conduct ourselves like Bais Hillel when Mashiach will come the halacha will be in accordance with Bais Shammai and we will light eight on the first night.

WHEN WE LIGHT THE CANDLES

42. The Gemorah tells us that we light the candles "from the time the sun sets." There is a debate as to whether this means the beginning of what we call sundown or whether it means when three medium stars appear. Practically speaking, Rav Moshe Feinstein zatzal held that we light 13 to 18 minutes after sunset. Rav Aharon Kotler held that we light 25-30 minutes after sundown.

43. When one will be unable to light later, one may light as early as Plag Mincha which is 1 and ¼ halachic hours before sunset. Generally, in New York City, this is sometime between 3:30 PM and 3:37 PM.

WHERE WE LIGHT THE CANDLES

44. In the time of Chazal, the Minhag was to light the Menorah outside by the entranceway facing the street. However, when Jews started living among the gentiles the Minhag changed to light in the house on account of danger. Now the main Pirsumei Nissah is for the family members. The question arises as to why we do not go back to the original custom in situations where, thank G-d, there is no longer danger. The Aruch haShulchan answers that the weather would extinguish the Menorah and Chazal did not go so far as to demand that we enclose the Menorah in glass. In Eretz Yisroel today many people do light outside in a glass enclosed case.

45. One may not light the Menorah above twenty Amos (28 feet 4 inches according to R. Feinstein zt"l). If a person lives on the first, second or third floor of an apartment building it is ideal to place the Menorah by the window because there is still Pirsumei Nissah for passerbyers on the street.

46. If one lives on the fourth floor or above it is preferable to place the Menorah next to the entrance of the apartment.

47.Remember, for people who live below the fourth floor including in a house, it is preferable to place the Menorah next to the window, rather than next to the entrance. When we do place the Menorah next to the entrance we place it on the side opposite the Mezuzah so that we are surrounded by Mitzvos. It is placed next to the doorway so that people will realize that the owner purposefully placed it there.

48.Ideally the Menorah should be at least three tefachim handbreadths above the ground and below ten handbreadths. The reason why it should be above three tefachim is because some people place things on the floor and it may not be recognizable that it was done for Pirsumei Nissah. The reason why it should be below ten handbreadths is that lights used for seeing purposes are usually placed above three feet high.

49.Three handbreadths amount to 10.62 inches and ten handbreadths are 35.4 inches. The ten Tefachim requirement is measured from the flame not the Menorah. The three handbreadth requirement is from the base not the flame.

50.If there are any safety issues involved in placing it below or above these recommended heights, safety precautions should be followed first. If there are little children or grandchildren in the house access to the

Menorahs should be blocked. Couches and or other things that are easily flammable should be placed at a far distance from the Menorah.

WHO IS OBLIGATED?

51.Everyone is obligated in lighting – men, women, and children who have reached the age of instruction. Women are obligated because they too were involved in the miracle. Unless they have a minhag otherwise, however, married women and single girls should preferably fulfill their Mitzvah with the Baal HaBayis. The Chsam Sofer explains that in previous times everyone lit outside. Back then it would have been a breach in Tznius for women to go outside and light. Even though nowadays we light indoors, most women still maintain the original practice and rely upon the lighting of the Baal HaBayis.

52.If for some reason the man cannot light, a woman may light for him and be Motzi him.

53.What is considered the age of instruction? The Pri MaGadim writes in his preface that for most Mitzvos other than Shmah and Tefillah the age of instruction is 5 or 6 depending upon the sharpness of the child. If the child understands things earlier then he should be given a Menorah to light. The Mishna Brurah notes that one does not have to give a child more than one candle to light on any given night. Common custom nowadays is to let the child light the full amount of candles.

WITH WHAT TO LIGHT

54.The ideal method of lighting is with olive oil – even though one may light with any type of oil or candles. Olive oil is ideal because the miracle actually happened with olive oil. If at first someone did not have olive oil and set up the menorah with wax candles, and then the olive oil arrived – one should use the wax candles and not the olive oil.

55.One may reuse the wicks used during the previous night. This is not a bizayon to the Mitzvah at all – it actually makes it easier to light the Menorah.

56.It is important to beautify our Mitzvos because of the posuk – "*Zeh Kaili veAnveihu* – This is my L-rd and I shall glorify him." This applies to Rabbinic Mitzvos as well. One should therefore try to purchase a nice Menorah. Many people use a silver Menorah for this reason.

57.It is proper to make sure that the flames of each of the Chanukah candles are the same height.

58.A metal or glass Menorah is preferable to other types of Menorah because of Hiddur Mitzvah – beautifying the Mitzvah. Many Poskim write that metal is preferable to glass. A candelabra, although technically permitted for Chanukah Menorah use, is not considered a Hiddur Mitzvah for Chanukah.

59.An electric Menorah has neither a wick nor oil and may not be used as a Chanukah menorah. If a person is a patient in a hospital and cannot light any other way, some Poskim hold that the patient should not light with an electric Menorah. Rabbi Ovadiah Yoseph writes that in such circumstances one should use an electric Menorah but should not recite a blessing.

THE BRACHOS WE RECITE

60.On the first night of Chanukah three blessings are recited immediately prior to the lighting: 1] Lehadlik ner shelchanukah 2] Sheasa Nissim laAvosainu and 3] Shehecheyanu. The third bracha is not recited on the other nights. However, if one forgot to recite the

Shehecheyanu on the first night, he or she should recite it on the next night that it is remembered.

61. There are three versions of the blessing of Lehadlik: Some say, "Lehadlik ner Chanukah." Others say, "Lehadlik ner shel Chanukah." The third option, which is the one recommended by the Mishna Brurah, is that "shelchanukah" is one word.

EREV SHABBOS & MOTZEI SHABBOS

62. On Erev Shabbos we light the Chanukah candles before the Shabbos candles. Enough oil must be placed in the menorah to ensure that the lights last ½ hour into the night. Regular Chanukah candles will not work unless they are frozen for at least 4 hours beforehand.

63. It is preferable to daven Mincha before lighting the Chanukah candles but a man should not miss minyan on this account.

64. The candles cannot be lit before Plag Mincha which at its earliest is 3:30 PM in New York and may go until 3:37 PM.

65. On Motzei Shabbos, the general minhag in our homes is to say Havdallah first and then light the Chanukah candles. The reason is that Havdallah is

more Tadir – more common than Chanukah candles. In shul, however, the Chanukah candles are lit first and then Havdallah is recited. The person who lights in shul does not fulfill his obligation to light at home – neither on Motzei Shabbos or during the week.

WHEN NOT AT HOME

66.Sometimes the halachos of where one lights can get very complex and a Rav should be consulted when a person is not at home. The issue revolves around one's Kvius. The rule of thumb is that if one will return home that evening you light when you get home. If one had spent the night before at that place then one may light there even if one will return home later. Lighting at a Bar Mitzvah or wedding is not acceptable and is considered a Bracha Levatalah.

TEFILOS ON CHANUKAH

67.We add the special Tefillah of Al HaNissim to every Shmoneh Esreh of Chanukah. We also add it to our benching throughout Chanukah. If it was left out, however, it is not repeated.

68.We recite the complete Hallel each day of Chanukah. The reason is because a miracle occurred each and every day of Chanukah.

69.Since the Mishkan was completed on the 25th of Kislev we read the parsha of the gifts of the Nesiim each day of Chanukah from the Torah during Shacharis. This also alludes to the promise that Hashem gave to Aharon and the Leviim about the Chanukah lights lasting forever.

70.Chanukah comes out on the following days in these years:

2011: December 20-28

2012: December 8-16

2013: November 27-December 5

2014: December 16-24

2015: December 6-14

Chapter Two - Purim

Before Purim

1. It is important to know that the entire experience of Adar and Purim should be a time where one undergoes tremendous and remarkable growth in both Avodas Hashem and Dveikus Bashem. Whoever does not experience this growth has failed to fully appreciate Purim and what it could bring about.

2. The Gemorah (Taanis 29a) tell us that when the Month of Adar begins we increase our joyous activity. Why is this so? Because this month is a very favorable time for the Jewish people.

3. The miracles of Purim occurred in the Hebrew years 3404 and 3405, after the first Beis HaMikdash was destroyed and five years before the second Beis HaMikdash was built in 3410. Achasveirosh's feast was in 3395 and Esther had been taken to Achashveirosh in 3399. She was Queen for six years before the miracle of Purim occurred.

4. The Meshech Chochma explains that Esther's original plan was to give up her own life in order to save the Jewish people. She planned that Achashveirosh would kill both her and Haman, and that Achashveirosh would undo everything that Haman was planning to do. She was willing to sacrifice her life and her reputation forever so that Klal Yisroel would continue to exist. Because Esther was willing to do this, and on account of Klal Yisroel's remarkable Teshuvah, Hashem changed the plan. Esther's life and reputation would not be sacrificed. Hashem could not allow that. And this time would forever onward be a time of goodwill and fortune for Klal Yisroel. It is also important to remember that this was a salvation brought about on account of a remarkable level of Ahavas Yisroel.

5. Rav Dessler in his Michtav M'Eliyahu explains that time is not a straight flow of a river. Rather, it flows in a circle, like a carousel. Special events that occurred to the Jewish people in the past leave a mark on that very day, whenever it comes up again in the future. Purim is a time when Hashem is particularly close to the Jewish people. During this time, Hashem saved us from destruction.

6. We, the nation of Israel, drew ourselves ever closer to Hashem. The closeness was so visible for all to see that even gentiles observed it and jumped to convert and join us. Indeed, Chazal explain that on Purim, Hashem is so close to us, that even Yom Kippurim is called – like Purim.

7. Therefore, the Mogain Avrohom writes, if one has a lawsuit with an idol-worshipper, a special effort should be made to settle it during the month of Adar.

The Four Parshios

8. There are four special Parshios that Chazal instituted to read in addition to the regular Parsha HaShavuah to read as Maftir. These four special maftirs are read beginning from before the month of Adar until the month of Nissan. These parshios assist us in developing the very special Kesher we have with HaKadosh Boruch Hu during these two months.

9. The first Parsha of the four is Parshas Shekalim. This Parsha brings to mind the half shekel that the Jewish people brought in order to bring the Korban Tamid – the sacrifices brought daily in the Bais HaMikdash. It is proper to realize that term "sacrifice" is

a mistranslation. The correct translation of "Korban" is "a closifier" – or "something that brings one closer to Hashem."

10. The next parsha is Parshas Zachor, which causes us to remember the actions of Amalek. It is a Torah Mitzvah to recall his actions and to abhor him with a hate firmly situated in the heart. We read it during this time because Haman was a descendent of Amalek, and Hashem saved us from him.

11. If one did not hear Parshas Zachor on this Shabbos, he may fulfill the Mitzvah by listening to the Torah reading that is read on the morning of Purim which discusses Moshe Rabbeinu's war with Amalek. . However, he must specifically have in mind that he is fulfilling the Mitzvah of Parshas Zachor at this time. He must also request of the Baal Koreh that he specifically have in mind to be Motzi him. If either of these two requirements are not fulfilled, he has not fulfilled his Mitzvah.

12. The third parsha is Parshas Parah which commemorates the Parah Adumah that was prepared in the desert after the Mishkan was erected so that the Korban Pesach could be eaten in purity. We read it now so that Hashem should throw this purifying

water upon us as well – speedily in our days. Some say that it is a Torah Mitzvah to read this Parsha as it is part of the Mitzvah to remember the sin of the Aigel HaZahav.

13. The fourth Parsha is Parshas HaChodesh which is read to sanctify the month of Nissan. Nissan is the time when we both dedicated the Mishkan and when we became the Am Hashem.

14. These four Parshios are read in addition to the weekly Torah portion but they replace the regular Maftir read after the seventh Aliyah..

15. The determination of when these parshios are read is dictated by the need for Parshas Zachor being read immediately before Purim and Parshas HaChodesh being read immediately prior to Rosh Chodesh Nissan.

Taanis Esther

16. During the time of Mordechai and Esther the Jews united on the 13th of Adar – to fight and wage war thus standing up for their lives. They fasted during the day of the battle to beseech mercy from Hashem. Hashem sees and hears every person in his or

her time of need, when they fast and return to Hashem with all their heart. In order to remember that Hashem does this, all of Israel accepted upon themselves this fast of Esther.

17. Esther herself fasted for three days, but she did so during the month of Nissan. However, since Nissan is the special month when we were redeemed and it is also when the Mishkan was erected – Chazal made the observation of the fast in Adar.

18. Taanis Esther is not as obligatory as the four written fasts found in the Neviim. When necessary, therefore, one can be lenient such as for expecting or nursing women, or if someone has a severe headache or something similar. Others, however, should not separate themselves from the community and should fast. The custom among some different groups in Klal Yisroel for the women not to fast is entirely incorrect and should be stopped.

19. According to Rav Moshe Feinstein zt"l, if a person is having difficulty fasting, he or she may eat a small amount of food 41 minutes after Shekiya before the Megillah reading.

20. When reading the Torah at Mincha of Taanis Esther, only those that are fasting may receive an Aliyah.

If there is no Levi that is present who is fasting, the Kohain is called twice.

21.The holiday of Purim was split into two days – because the salvation and fighting that occurred in the capital of Persia, Shushan happened on an additional day. It happened on the 14th and the 15th of Adar. Since Shushan was a walled city, the sages of the time decreed that every walled city should celebrate Purim a day later. Jerusalem is a walled city and Purim is celebrated on the 15th of Adar not the 14th. For the honor of Eretz Yisroel the determination of what is a walled city was set back to the time of Yehoshua.

Machtzis HaShekel

22.Immediately before Purim, it is the custom to give half shekels of the established coinage of the country to charity in order to commemorate the half shekels that were given for the communal sacrifices. These were done in Adar. We give three half shekels because in parshas Ki Sisah, where the matter of the donation is discussed, the word Trumah appears three times.

23.The money given for Machtzis HaShekel should be aside from the amount given each year for Maaser. Some say that ideally the money should be given to the maintenance of the shul,the Yeshiva, or the Bais Ha-Midrash.

24.A child is not obligated in Machtzis HaShekel. Some say that the obligation begins at thirteen. Others rule that it is at twenty. If a father gave Machtzis haShekel for a child even once, he is obligated to continue doing so each year.

25.Women are exempt from the Mitzvah of Machtzis HaShekel. Although the Talmud Yerushalmi discusses the apparent obligation of women giving Machtzis HaShekel, the reference refers only to women who have taken the Mitzvah upon themselves voluntarily.

26.If one neglected to give the Machtzis HaShekel immediately before Purim, he may do so until Rosh Chodesh Nissan.

The Tefilos on Purim

27.In the Shmoneh Esreh of Maariv, Shacharis, and Minchah and in Bentching we add the Tefillah of Al

HaNissim. The Mishna Brurah writes that the correct Nussach is to add a vov in the beginning, as in, "V'al HaNissim." This is both in Davening as well as in Bentching.

28. If Al HaNissim was forgotten, one does not have to rerecite either the davening or the bentching. The Mishna Brurah recommends inserting it as a request in Elokai Netzor found at the end of Shmoneh Esreh. It is proper to place a piece of paper in the Siddur to remind ourselves to recite Al HaNissim.

29. One should not eat before hearing the Megillah unless it is very necessary. "Very necessary" means that one is either sick or has difficulty with not eating. The reason why such an issue is made of the reading of the Megillah is because of the importance of this Mitzvah - it pushes off all other Mitzvos. Women should also not eat before hearing the Megillah.

30. One may, however, have a coffee in the morning before the reading of the Megillah. It is also permitted to add sugar.

31. Hallel is not recited on Purim because the reading of the Megillah is itself considered a recitation of song. If one does not have a Megillah and will not

hear the reading from a Megillah, the Poskim have ruled that hallel should be said, but without a blessing.

Reading the Megillah

32. The obligation is to read the Megillah at night and in the day in commemoration of the miracle, where they cried out day and night. The daytime reading begins at sunrise and continues until the end of the day. If it was read from Amud HaShachar – dawn, the Mitzvah has still been fulfilled.

33. The nighttime reading begins when three stars come out and continues throughout the night until 1 and 1/5th hours before sunrise.

34. If one lives far away and can only travel to hear one reading of the Megillah, it is preferable to hear the day reading rather than the night reading.

35. The most preferred manner of fulfilling the Mitzvah is to read the Megillah publicly, and in the Synagogue. When attending the Megillah in a bigger place one should have in mind that he or she is giving greater glory to Hashem by hearing the Megillah there. This Kavannah serves to bring us closer to Hashem,

and is an action similar in purpose to the recitation of Kaddish, an extremely holy endeavor.

Pirsumei Nissah

36.Reading the Megillah involves the notion of Pirsumei Nissah – publicizing the miracle. Because of this, it sets aside any other Mitzvah – even a Torah Mitzvah. Even the study of the Torah is set aside for the reading of the Megillah. The only Mitzvah which is not pushed off is the Mitzvah of providing burial for a dead person, when there is no one else available to do so. This is interesting because reading the Megillah is only a Rabbinic Mitzvah. If the other Mitzvah cannot be performed later, however, and it is a Biblical Mitzvah – that Mitzvah would come first. A Bris Milah is an exception to this halacha. The Bris Milah is performed before the reading of the Megillah.

37.Even if there are many people in one's company, he should not read the Megillah at home, but should rather go to the Synagogue, since, 'In a multitude there is Majesty;' and the miracle is made known more widely.

The Brachos on the Megillah

38.Before reading it, the reader of the Megillah recites these three blessings:

• "Al Mikrah Megillah" - Who sanctified us with His commandments, and commanded us with the Reading of the Megillah

• "Sh'asah nissim laAvosainu," - Who made miracles for our fathers in those days at this time...

• "Shehecheyanu." - Who kept us alive and sustained us...

After the reading he recites the blessing of "Harav es riveinu" - Who waged our quarrels...

39.The reader should intend to fulfill the obligation of the congregation. The congregation answers 'Amen,' and they too should intend to fulfill the Mitzvah. "Baruch Hu u'varuch Sh'mo' – is not said.

40.The only difference between the day reading and the night reading is that in the day when saying "Shehecheyanu" the Reader should have in mind the other Mitzvos of the day - the Purim Feast, the Sending of Gifts, and possibly Matanos L'Evyonim - Giving of Gifts to the Poor. Some leave out the last one possibly because it may be improper to recite a blessing on someone's misfortune.

41. If someone read it without having recited the blessings he has still fulfilled the Mitzvah. If a person remembered that the blessings were not recited, they may be recited in between the chapters of the Megillah.

42. If one reads the Megillah alone, he recites the "brachos" which come before it, but not the one which comes after. If one has already fulfilled the obligation of reading the Megillah, and he wishes to read it a second time for many other people, he recites all the "brachos" the beginning ones and the end bracha.

43. If he is reading the Megillah only for one other individual, he recites only the first brachos. If that person knows the brachos well, he says them himself.

44. Before HaRav es Riveinu - the final brachah after the Megillah Reading, the Megillah is rolled together. This is because it is disrespectful to keep the Megillah open after the reading.

Aspects of the Megillah

45. The Baal Koreh stops and waits for the Kahal four times during the reading. Where is this done? It is done during the four "verses-of-redemption." After he stops everyone listening reads the Pasuk before him. The Chazan then repeats it from his Megillah. This is because all the listeners are required to hear the entire Megillah read.

46. These are the four Psukim where he stops: "Ish Yehudi haya beshushan habirah - There was a Jew in Shushan the capital...' 'And Mordechai went forth from before the King in royal garments...' 'Unto the Jews there was light...' 'For Mordechai, the Jew, was second to the King. . .'

47. The purpose of this custom is to keep the children from slumber so that the great miracle performed for Israel in the days of Mordechai and Esther, might enter their hearts.

48. Another minhag is to read more loudly the Pasuk which states, "That night the sleep of the King was disturbed." It is also read in a slightly different tune. These changes are made because it is in this particular pasuk in which the salvation of the Jews actually be-

gins. According to the Kaballah, "the King" refers metaphorically to Hashem Himself.

49. We also read the names of the ten sons of Haman all together in one breath. This is also done with the four preceding words ['500 men and'], and the word 'ten' which follows the ten names. This is done to show that they were all killed and hung together. If this was not done the Mitzvah of reading has still been fulfilled.

50. Rav Michel Ber Weismandel zatzal, after the horrors of the Second World War, made a remarkable discovery in the letters of the Megillah itself. In the writing of the ten sons of Haman Megillah (9:7-9), there are three letters, the Taf, the Shin, and the Zayin, of a much smaller size than the other letters of the Megillah. These letters correspond to 5707 - the Hebrew year that occurred during the 1946 hangings that resulted after the Nuremburg Trials. Ten "sons of Haman" were hung during this period. No other adequate explanation has ever been given to explain the different sizes of the letters in this section. There is also a very large Hey in this section which corresponds to the fifth millennium (5000 plus 707).

51. It is interesting to note that Esther says in the Megillah, "Im al haMelech Tov, yiten gam lamachar es aseres Bnei Haman.. – If it is pleasing to the King, He should also give tomorrow – the ten sons of Haman. As mentioned before the Kaballah states that whenever the word HaMelech appears in the Megillah, it also refers metaphorically to Hashem. It is also interesting to note that Newsweek magazine reported that Julius Streicher, Yimach Shmo, one of ten Nazis hung at Nuremberg said while going to the gallows, the words "Purimfest, 1946!"

52. All are obligated in reading the Megillah: Men, women, converts, and children. The term "reading the Megillah" is used instead of "hearing the Megillah" for a reason. The obligation, however, is to hear it from someone who is himself obligated in reading it too.

Matanos L'Evyonim

53. There is a Mitzvah on Purim to give at least one gift to two different poor people on Purim day. Even a poor person himself has reached a financial state that he must ask for Charity, he must still give.

54.This obligation may be fulfilled through any type of gift - money, food, drink, or clothing. One should, however, try to give a substantial monetary gift. If one does use money, ideally it should be enough to buy bread weighing at least three eggs – five slices approximately. At the very least, however, one must give a pruta (now 3 cents) or its equivalent value to each of two poor persons. A pruta is 1/1244th of an ounce of silver – now valued at $35.44 per ounce. Rav Shmuel Kaminetsky shlita rules that the minimum amount should be one dollar.

55.These gifts should be given in the daytime. It should be given after the Megillah is read. Matanos L'Evyonim should be above and beyond Maaser.

56.Money set aside for Matanos L'Evyonim should not be changed to another Tzedaka without a ruling from a Posaik.

57.One is not overly strict with the poor on Purim to determine whether they are really poor or not. Whoever puts his hand out – we give him. According to leading Poskim, this does not apply to organizations, however.

58.Women are also obligated to give gifts to the poor on Purim. A married woman may fulfill the

Mitzvah through her husband. Ideally, however, the husband should inform his wife that he has given Matanos L'Evyonim for her as well.

59.Children relying on their parents' table should still give Matanos L'Evyonim on their own (Aruch HaShulchan 694:2).

60.Rav Moshe Feinstein zatzal ruled that one may fulfill the Mitzvah of Matanos L'Evyonim with a check. This is true even if the check is post-dated.

61.One may fulfill the Mitzvah of Matanos L'Evyonim by giving the money even to a young child who is considered poor.

62.Matanos L'Evyonim may be given anonymously. This is also the ideal form of fulfilling the Mitzvah.

63.There is a debate as to whether it is preferable to give many poor people a minimum amount of Matanos L'Evyonim or to give just a few people a significant amount of Matanos L'Evyonim. The Bach (Siman 695) writes that it is preferable to give more people the lesser amount. Rav Elyashiv Shlita is quoted (Shvus Yitzchok 8:2 as cited in Kovetz Halachos p. 92) that it is preferable to give fewer people a more significant amount. Since either way one fulfills the Mitzvah, one should perform it in the manner in which one feels most inspired toward Dveikus Bashem.

The Mitzvah of Mishloach Manos

64. It is also an obligation to send a gift of at least two portions of food to a friend. Men and women are both included in this Mitzvah.

65. There is no need for the two different food items to have two separate brachos. This is one of the biggest misconceptions in Hilchos Purim.

66. The Mitzvah must be fulfilled only with foods that are immediately edible or drinkable. An item that requires further cooking or preparation may be added, but two immediately usable foods must be included too. It is praiseworthy to send portions to as many friends as possible. It is better, however, to give more Matanos l'evyonim than to give more Mishloach Manos to friends.

67. Even a poor person is required to fulfill the Mitzvah of Mishloach Manos. The Mitzvah of Mishloach Manos may not be fulfilled with money, clothing, or other non-food or non-drink items. The Mitzvah may only be fulfilled with kosher items.

68.It is proper to send portions sufficient to convey regard for the recipient. One should not send something below the Kavod of the recipient. The Poskim have ruled that a lollipop is not considered Choshuv for an adult, nor is a bottle of Poland Spring or seltzer.

69.Virtually all the Poskim rule that a goy or a child may be a shliach for Mishloach Manos. Rabbi Akiva Eiger was unsure of this, however.

70.Ideally, Mishloach Manos should be sent through a messenger, rather than to be delivered personally. Generally speaking we say, "Mitzvah bo yoser mibeshlucho" it is a bigger Mitzvah to do it oneself rather than through a messenger. For the search for Chametz on Pesach it is better to do it oneself. Here though it is different. The Pasuk says, "Mishloach Manos" which indicates that it should be done through a messenger. A gift sent through a messenger is fancier and nicer. If one did deliver the Mishloach Manos oneself, the obligation is still fulfilled.

71.One does not fulfill the Mitzvah of Mishloach Manos with an anonymous gift.

The Purim Seudah

72.It is a Mitzvah to have a festive meal on Purim. It is during this meal that one experiences the most profound growth and escalation in our connection to HaKadosh Boruch Hu. This meal should include meat and wine.

73.This meal is held during the day. If one holds it at night, he has failed to fulfill his obligation. Nevertheless, one's evening meal should be more festive than usual. One should wear festival clothing and rejoice.

74.The main Purim meal is held Purim afternoon and is preceded by Minchah. The meal is extended into the night. Most of the meal, however, should be during the day.

75.When Purim falls on Friday, the meal is held early, and is finished with enough time before Shabbos that one will have a good appetite for the Shabbos meal. Some, however, have the custom to extend the meal until Shabbos arrives.

Drinking

76.The Biur Halacha poses the question as to why
drinking is a part of Purim when we find so many
Psukim that show how terrible and evil getting drunk
actually is. He explains that the miracles of Purim
actually all occurred through wine. A] Vashti was
removed from her throne because of wine. B] Haman
was brought down through wine. C]The Teshuvah of
Klal Yisroel involved regretting having drunk wine at
the feast of Achashveirosh.

77.Chazal enacted that those who truly experience
growth in Avodas Hashem should drink wine on
Purim. They said, "Chayav adam libsumei B'Puraya
ad de lo yada bain Arur Haman u Baruch Mordechai."
The Nesivus Shalom explains this to mean that a person is obligated to become genuinely intoxicated with
the notion of Purim – that is that no matter how distant
we are from Hashem – Hashem is close to us. Whether
throughout the year we are Boruch Mordechai or Arur
Haman – Hashem wants to develop our connection
with Him.

78.In terms of an actual obligation, the Ramah explains that it is sufficient to drink just a little more than

is his usual habit, and to take a nap. When one takes a nap the lack of consciousness creates a situation where one does not know the difference between Haman and Mordechai.

Working on Purim

79.It is technically permitted to work on Purim. Nonetheless, if possible, it should be avoided. The Ramah writes (OC chapter 696) that nowadays the custom is to refrain from working on Purim. Chazal tell us that "Whoever works on Purim does not see a siman bracha from it - any sign of blessing." This refers to work that involves making money or stre- nuous effort. Therefore, one may do machine laundry on Purim. One should avoid doing laundry by hand on Purim. One may therefore shave, get a haricut or cut one's nails on Purim.

80.The custom to refrain from work on Purim refers to the daytime, but not the evening, according to the Biur Halacha (written by the Chofetz Chaim).

81.Work involving a Mitzvah is completely permit- ted.

Mourning

82.Eulogies and fasting are forbidden Purim. If someone is a mourner rachmana litzlan, and is in Shiva, he or she does not publicly display mourning on Purim. Mourners do not sit on the ground nor remove their shoes. Private aspects of mourning are observed, however, just like on Shabbos.

83.Mourners must give Mishloach Manos but should not receive.

Marriage

84.It is permitted to get married on Purim and to have the wedding feast on this day as well. Although it has been a debate in the past, the Mishna Brurah permits it and writes that our custom is to allow it.

Adar Rishon

85.Purim is always celebrated in the second Adar if there are two Adars that year. [There is a second Adar seven times every nineteen years (3rd year, 6th year, 8th year, 11th year, 14th year, 17th year, and the 19th year). The last nineteen year cycle started in the year 5758 (that was year one). 5771 is the 14th year. This calendar is called the Guach Luach.]

86.However, on the 14th and 15th of Adar Rishon we do not fast or make eulogies. The custom is not to do other things during this time. Some do have the custom to increase eating and joy on the 14th. In order to fulfill all opinions, however, it is best to increase the meal a little bit.

Purim Falling on Sunday

87.When Purim falls on Sunday, Taanis Esther is pushed up earlier and is observed on Thursday. This is because the day before Purim is Shabbos and we do not fast then. It is permitted, however, for the Baal Koreh to practice reading the Megillah on this Shabbos, because it is still considered Torah study.

88.It is nonetheless forbidden to bring a copy of the Megillah on Shabbos day in preparation for the Saturday night reading of the Megillah even when there is an Eiruv. This is considered Hachana on Shabbos for during the week.

Personal Miracle

89.If someone was the beneficiary of a personal miracle, he may institute upon himself and his descendents a personal day of Purim. We rule that such a meal is considered a Seudas Mitzvah since it is done to commemorate the wonders that Hashem performed for us. Certainly, the members of a community or city may enact such a community Purim – as long as the members of that community or city had accepted it upon themselves. The Chayei Odom and his descendents celebrate the 15th of Kislev as their personal Purim on account of the fact that his family was miraculously saved from a fire on that day. They fast on the 15th and on that evening they light candles, recite the Shir HaKavod, and make a feast.

90.The idea of a personal Purim reflects the notion that all of a person's experiences in life should serve the purpose of bringing us to an ever higher level of devotion and Dveikus Bashem.

CPSIA information can be obtained at www.ICGtesting.com
Printed in the USA
BVOW08s0045120315

391371BV00018B/161/P